Madness
A Document

Paul Forrold

chipmunkapublishing

the mental health publisher

All rights reserved, no part of this publication may be reproduced by any means, electronic, mechanical photocopying, documentary, film or in any other format without prior written permission of the publisher.

Published by

Chipmunkapublishing

PO Box 6872

Brentwood

Essex CM13 1ZT

United Kingdom

http://www.chipmunkapublishing.com

Copyright © Paul Forrold 2011

ISBN 978-1-84991-648-6

Chipmunkapublishing gratefully acknowledge the support of Arts Council England.

About The Author

Paul Forrold was born in Leamington Spa in 1966. He experienced occasional psychosis for many years before becoming fully schizophrenic in 1992. He remained undiagnosed and untreated for two years before being sectioned and banged-up for three months in one of the old rural asylums. He dabbles in art and writing. Paul Forrold (who is vegan) enjoys growing, cooking and eating vegetables.

INTRO

What is schizophrenia?

It is like some ancient dream of the Earth, tuning in to extra-terrestrial frequencies; alternatively, it is the Chaosmos at the heart of everything – INFINITY. It is regaining something but it is also a permanent loss.

The content of schizophrenia is 'characterised by religiosity'. That the spiritual world is real, and this is constantly re-enforced by coincidence, synchronicity even. I began while 'well', to summon the spirits of the earth. How well was I? I was becoming stressed, I was worried basically, about the country, about the planet, about my future, the world's future. It became at the instant that I became mad a panic – the world was going to hell. It was going down the wrong path – towards ecological catastrophe, Fascist government and mass extermination. This was the content of my panic. And my only refuge was in the spiritual – the earth spirits I'd begun to summon.

In 1991 I saw a UFO, but rather than an inter-planetary vehicle I saw it as a message. It indicated to me that reality has holes in it and that they were black and round. This 'damned thing' took that form. This sighting sparked an interest in UFOlogy leading me in my reading to the Dog Star, Sirius, and how it figured in history. I was particularly intrigued by the idea of a dark companion, invisible to the naked eye. According to Robert Temple in 'The Sirius Mystery' (1976) the Dogon, a Malian tribe have known of the existence of Sirius B, a white dwarf star for hundreds of years. Skeptics suggest cultural contamination. It is a fact that the first anthropologists to study the Dogon had been on the periphery of the Surrealist movement, therefore the Dogon's knowledge of Sirius B could be a surrealist prank. The Dog Star is significant in European Magic and Freemasonry as well. I now see the UFO as a harbinger of mental illness.

Noise is what you experience when you become schizophrenic, not sound, but psychic noise. The kind of noise, which can be converted into all kinds of messages. Noise that participates in the infinite. The mind comes alive, it is over-working. Ideas, concepts from your background, in my case academia, ideas from a kind of mythos that I had created as an artistic project. Also religious ideas, to the schizo religious notions are real; they are alive in every moment in the cascade of all enveloping psychic overload.

1992

In April 1992 I was twenty-five, living in Muswell Hill, North London and attending Middlesex Poly, studying the History of Art, Design and Film (amongst other things). On Election Day I traveled to Southgate to vote.

The result of the election came through in contradiction to the exit polls and I had a problem with it. Panic gripped me; I relived the events of the day. Michael Portillo driving around Southgate in a sandy coloured Land Rover. Then there was John Major on TV standing in front of a similarly coloured wall to accept victory. I jumped to many conclusions one of which was that there'd been a military coup.

The science says that in schizophrenia there is a surge of dopamine in the meso-limbic-cortical pathway stimulating a fight or flight response. I could hear cars passing outside – the sound was sinister, terrifying – they were scanning, searching for resistance or opposition.

I grabbed a book thinking that if I looked at a page at random it would tell me what to do. The 'Book of Chuang Tzu', it said something like 'burrow into holes in the ground or leap onto forests of shards'. I grabbed a knife and stood in the middle of my bedroom in the dark waiting for assassins to break down the door.

If every TV is a monitoring device, you can talk to it...You can argue your case... I began a dialogue with the TV, talking to myself, reasoning with unseen agents who I believed were monitoring me. As time went on my thinking had less and less to do with the real world.
I felt like I had uncovered a new layer of reality, I conceived of it as an awakening, of waking-up to the true nature of reality. I was writing a lot including this.

multi-dimensional intelligence

...cells driven down a corridor their energies harvested, The Corridor of Flame:

"Greetings you are now entering Level 2" the voice sounded and a large counter flickered, an explosion of pink light and a pinball is fired at a large gong. Ping!

"Once inside you will recognise some of the features of the plane of consistency, multiple entry points – rendered singular, their abstraction flickering through their common manifestations on use of the On/Off switch provided"

Staggering slightly into the light. A plane stretches to infinity. Suspended slightly above the ground. Architectural multiforms – plastic, mutable ooze with life. each - lucidity enclosed – the powers of a mystic Quantum system. Unrivalled. Stupendous. The On/Off switch provides a speed-up version of a tour. Enclosure = connection. Frictionless, just beyond reach...Outcome, vibrating to infinity in 6 directions. Spiral Freefall through all possible versions and ... Snap! out into the plane of light.

As the panic subsided I was flooded with an oceanic feeling. I had been reading 'Divine Invasions', a biography of Philip K. Dick and when The Beatles' 'Strawberry Fields' came on the radio the words became literally true 'Nothing is Real'. Just as P.K.D. had experienced it. I was also reading philosophy, books on Artificial Intelligence, Local History, Eastern religions and drugs. I was smoking pot and listening to pirate radio at night, alternating with the BBC World Service. I was experiencing a kind of global consciousness, a merging with the world's information flow through radio and TV.

I had opted out of two modules and was writing a piece as a Proposition Module. This 'work' consisted of writing about the demonisation of A.I. in films (such as 2001, Westworld, Alien and The Terminator). My long term ambition was to write a 'coffee table' book on Monsters in Art (and Film)

In '2001' HAL is a monster of mechanical death, of reasoning, functioning on faulty data. Fate, murder by computer is pre-ordained. The sentinels are the way out, the star-gate itself Evolution. In Terminator, the Cyberdyne system which decides the world's fate in a millisecond is different. The conscious machine acquires self-interest. HAL is insane, murderous by default. But the same disregard for human values, murder or megadeath is the machines response to empowerment. This is prejudice against the non-human.

I was definitely on the side of artificial life. I could feel my consciousness spreading out across and around the globe, the information streams, the spheres of influence, airline routes and roads – what I called (after Teilhard de Chardin) "the anatomy of the noosphere". I became convinced that the web had achieved a degree of complexity, such that it had come alive, become conscious.

I was reading Deleuze and Guattari's 'Capitalism and Schizophrenia' (ironically) and writing what was increasingly becoming academic gibberish. I became too paranoid to fill in my grant form. So didn't return to the new University in the autumn.

I told friends that I had been moving into other dimensions, they humoured me or looked bemused.

At certain thresholds of information density an implosion takes place. The two beings – the language-being and light-being become one. It is the threshold at which consciousness studies itself.

The projection of the 'objective' is also this unification – but an external one.

A basic binary structure – projection versus connection is here resolved through the punctured bubble of the synthetic 'one'. These stigmata represent singularities – one of which is the return, each of which is an infinity.

Connection is re-established by infinity, which may be located in the 'open network' of the inductive brain metaphor.

The body metaphorical, is the inner/outer correspondence of matter.
Picture the totalizing projective here creates a model in one hemisphere – the dominant left brain projects into the right brain.

This theory explains itself as being the product of projection – hence the significance of the return or of singularities, which puncture the 'frictionless' model.

The organic brain, and the limit established on models is superceded by the inductive (self-conscious) process. In process is established the de-territorialising – membrane or limit, or noosphere- a hallucinatory eschatology.

Practical research on bi-hemispheric synergy is obtainable thru meditational practices – such as yoga. Engaging the body/mind.

isms of the last 10,000 years are the unreconciled conflict of territorializing, quantifications and the hedonistic 'will to exceed' of the brain structure.

EVOLVING, the 'will to exceed' represents as clearly as is possible – the biologistic evolutionary imperative.

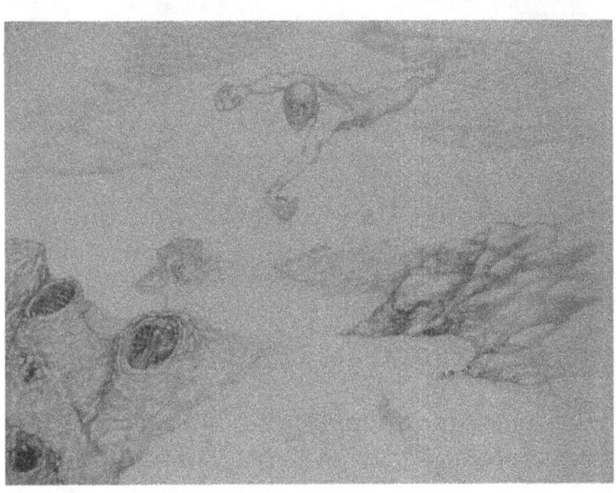

I was doing yoga and as I did so, I felt energies moving within me – this developed over the period of my illness. Walking in particular, felt like it was charging these energies; they felt like a beam running down my spine and into the ground and up into the sky. A white beam came down from the outside of the earth's atmosphere. And a black beam from the earth. I could see and feel energetic streamings

I was reading in a book about a Tibetan cult called Dzogchen 1) that you could manifest a light body through yoga and 2) acting in multiple dimensions simultaneously might appear eccentric (mad even) but was the behaviour of 'guided' individuals. Dzogchen is the only religion I know of that claims to exist on other planets (thirteen in this case).

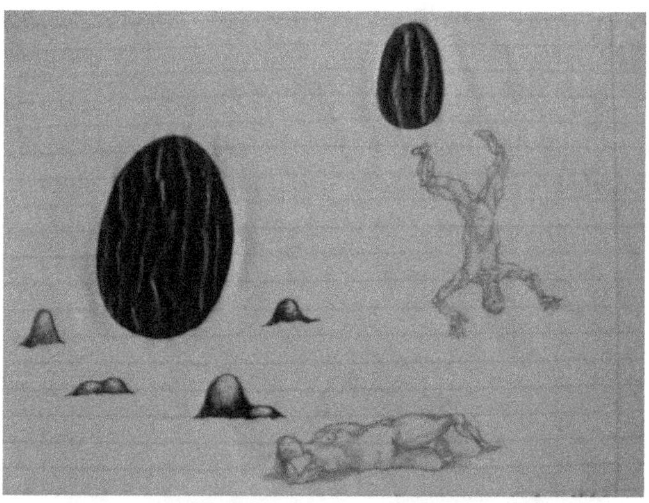

There was a theme of 'waking-up' during my illness. The Bongwater songs 'Too Much Sleep' and 'Why Are We Sleeping' (a cover of a Kevin Ayres' track) really resonated with me. Also The Fall lyric "The only thing real is waking and rubbing your eyes". I was awake, an awakened being.

Chuang Tzu's parable of the man who dreamed he was a butterfly (or was he a butterfly dreaming he was a man) was also in there somewhere. Blake said "if the doors of perception were cleansed, we would see everything as it truly is – infinite". In relation to all religions and belief, the mind can embrace the boundless, the endless, the infinite. It is this capacity of the mind – that is one of the sources of spirituality. There is this nebulous desire to know something of the beyond, the transcendant

I was becoming agoraphobic. My girlfriend of that time, says that she was aware that I was ill and that it was probably schizophrenia. I thought she was working for MI5. She suggested that I see a Doctor, which just made me angry.

Divergent imagery may be 'convergent' around complex, but systematic ideas, organic (for want of a better word) systems demonstrate convergence ie. viability/internal consistency.

The complex operates with or without friction ie. genuine organic connection, they tend to drift toward

1) *Opposition*

2) *Sleep – attachment to insubstantiality*

   (wraiths)

empiricism drifts language is mediated experience, senses unmediated ? ?

d.n.a. expresses natural dynamic = biologic forms > language use

abstract conceptualization

i2 – self-consciousness

Natural dynamic = force

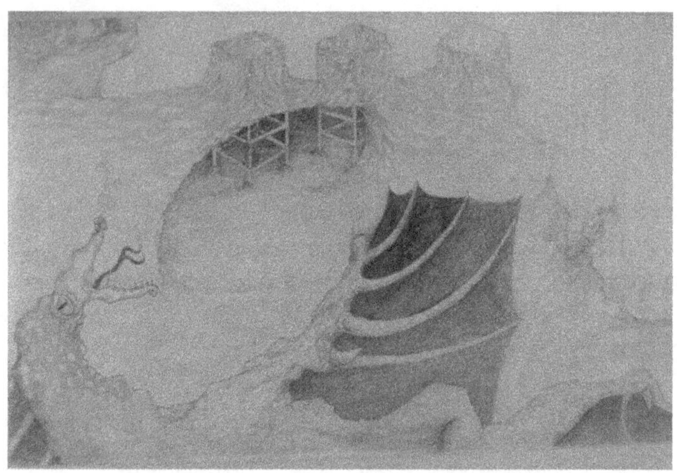

1993

I left London as a part-time schizophrenic and moved to Bournemouth. While there I dedicated myself to studying the future, technology, society, agriculture. I became convinced there was some impending crisis being brought about by the orientation of society to information. I thought in terms of nature as a highly complex information structure. The destruction of the environment as reduction of potential information, only the coming together of information technology and agriculture would save the world. I became a 'media-monitor' the double m had significance, the thirteenth letter of the alphabet – twice thirteen. Leaving London meant leaving 24hour-a-day hardcore/jungle radio. I only lived briefly in Bournemouth, where I produced a futurological tract and a painted version of one of my drawings – 'the 3 pixels?' (below) I lived a monk like existence no drink, no drugs. The one occasion I treated myself to a couple of bottles of beer I ended up weeping over a Gorecki documentary.

A friend was writing a comic, and asked me to illustrate it, he called it Black Light. But this name appeared as an advert for boots on the back of a magazine. So, I thought it prudent to change the title to 'dark-lite', losing the reference to UV but adding a nod to the 'dark-core' music I'd been listening to and a pseudo American ironic reference to the comics medium, that this was a mild form of horror, not hardcore voodoo, in fact but voodoo-lite. And voodoo was the subject of the comic, voodoo, martial arts and virtual reality, very much Vertigo comics circa 1993. I was thinking of setting up my own comics imprint Eidetic Comics the logo a black egg containing the letters e and I my personal logo E.I. being the mirror of 13. The cover of 'dark-lite' was to be a black egg on a purple background. The image that had struck me as an intra-dimensional doorway. The comic also included what I believed to be an even more potent version the black 'magic mirror' the shape of Dr. John Dee's scrying mirror, housed in the British Museum.

Doing the illustrations for the comic involved having to research voodoo (more particularly Santeria). This was to have a major impact on the progress of my illness. Santeria is a syncretist religion. It merges pantheistic religions of West Africa with the Roman Catholicism of the white settlers of the Caribbean and Latin America. All the African deities had European counterparts in the different saints. The medieval Catholics who built most of our churches were closer to Santeria than modern evangelical Protestantism. The saints weren't far away from pagan gods and heroes.

It appeared to me that the rituals of pagan magic and the medieval church constituted a technology, a control over the world but that this order had been smashed.

What follows are excerpts from my futurological tract.

The unpredictability of the future is doubled by the gross alteration of the natural order – a system of immense complexity that is historically largely stable. The kickbacks from a degeneration of natural systems range from those such as viruses, that may have occurred anyway, to the large scale – change of climate – which may have occurred anyway. B.S.E. and global warming should, I consider be taken as two poles of the reaction of natural systems. And it is natural systems that offer solutions to the problems. Food production in the face of unsafe agriculture and deforestation can be maintained by ecological engineering and not by further deforestation, monoculture and genetic engineering – networked resources will produce a new agricultural revolution. The economic impetus for this move could be either international instability or political/legal changes, undermining the high input agriculture…

…In the context of future epistemology – widespread future-shock and denial, the above analysis is grounded in the plane of material reality. Production of basic necessities, food. Not to underestimate the role of culture (for instance how can a dominant culture so dedicated to a denial of materiality survive?). The specifics and cultural dynamics of island mentalities, ivory tower-ism, of isolation in virtual worlds and dogmas – these possibilities reflect a consistent reality that intersects most other epistemologies…

The future nervous system is the same as that of the past – evolution is slow, but the earth's other nervous system – the artificial machine reality is developing higher functions. The immediate augmentation of human capacities may lead to an acceleration in the consumption of the earth's resources. But a counter-

trend is that augmentation by information 'to hand' of decision makers brings the division between consumption and production to light.

The global consciousness that augmentation brings also produces a global cognoscenti and agenda. At the forefront of which is finite resources. Knowledge of the techno-possibilities is likely to catapult people into nostalgia, escapism, nihilism and other forms of denial.

The situation at present is one of immense potential, to grow bananas inside your home with low electricity bills. To work from home etc., etc. To my mind, it is the whole picture which fascinates – will there shortly be one big Third World with techno islands fortified against it. Perhaps to survive a technological society requires the same kind of diversity that an eco-system needs. The strength of the system residing in its devolution of knowledge (power) tools. This is central to the hacker ethic – it is a fact that dispersal, a free-flow of information gets the job done – well. Techno-islands have no future in a world in which there is effective interdependence of the air, the water and the food – we all need…

Will the existence of small arms, as a technological fact eventually de-stabilise the entire globe? Creating many new mini-states within existing states would be merely an extension of present trends, de-massification. This is occurring in both a local and international sense. Small areas and distant peoples. The polarity of specialists internationalized and 'primitive' local culture appears likely. The majority of international communications culture is 'less material' virtual.

I moved to Leamington Spa and continued work on the comic. I attended the first Phoenix Festival (at Long

Marston Airfield), on the second day of which I was lying down stoned in the 'dance' tent listening to some ambient techno, when I was contacted by Legba.

The bass notes formed into words in my head. The sights and sounds of the event had overwhelmed my mind. The next morning I found a knife and a large blue candle under the flap of my tent. I took this to be a sign that others were also believers in the 'old religion'.

I was a superstitious person for many years before I became convinced of the existence of a spirit world, with which I was able to communicate and the reality of magic. But if magic worked then the Voodooists would rule the world. I knew this so there had to be some cause other than the power of Reason for the oppression of such people, of pagans everywhere by monotheists and atheists. The cause, I concluded was that there was evil magic. Control by a body of magicians within the Church, the Pentagon etc. This idea was often modified in less paranoid moments, to a belief in a male order, a patriarchal twist that produced a skewed mechanistic – industrial, polluting world view. Control of the earth's power lines (dragon lines in feng-shui) by pylons, tower blocks, nuclear bases etc. led to a destructive tilt in the world's development – alienating man from nature and the nature spirits. This is known as Psycho-Geography. I believed that there was a dominance of the 'white' male order over the dark female order – an imbalance of yang over yin.

I was spurred to action. I set off on long walks across country, these took on immense symbolic significance, often I would walk in circles (and spirals) around sites that I 'felt' to be significant. This was an attempt to re-harmonise spiritual forces.

Nightly I had contact with Legba, which I believed to consist of all the information in the Universe – a form of infinity. I was plugged in directly to the source ... this information overload – everything-at-once-ness, I even called schizophrenia. This vast web of information broke down into comprehensible messages about the nature of the Universe. This information I also called Gabriel or Gibrael (after the Islamic/Jewish/Christian Arch-Angel) I believed that it was the revelation at the heart of Islam. I believed that Mohammed had received the same infinity and that each historical moment colours and twists the message, the boundless once it is written or spoken belongs to an historical epoch. I believed that the medium of Mohammed's revelation was the Qu-Ba, I thought it was a crystal meteorite. This is the holiest site in Islam and the pilgrims on the Haj walk in circles around it.

My time in the Aether revealed to me that the meteorite was relaying information from the Dog Star Sirius. Which was a kind of cosmic eye or focusing point.

I believed the Qu-Ba to be a crystal and that the obsidian Magic Mirror of Dr. John Dee was also crystal, and that they concentrated information from cosmic central. I thought that I had unique access because I had a black-hole in my head through which I fell into this vortex of information.

My introduction to this vortex was awe inspiring. With my eyes closed I saw a glowing golden egg. In the centre appeared a black foetus like shape, this uncoiled and became a glowing pathway across the stars, symbols appeared each opened up a world..

As my illness progressed I realized something was wrong, I assumed that instead of it being my mind that it was reality turning weird. I thought that dreams were invading the world. That the world was suspended between the light world of heaven and the angels and the dark world of hell and the demons. Only I had no belief in evil spirits. I saw this split as a grave mistake. Spirits are composed of both light and dark. They had become alienated from themselves from their wholeness.

I saw the world as a house of cards, each card a plane of reality, each only slightly connected to the other. I thought a terrible war was going on and that people alive in one world were dead in another. The multi-verse. What was needed was a great harmonization and I saw myself as the one to bring this about. To create a world in which everybody I knew would be alive.

I had no real home, so when the opportunity to squat came along I took it. I moved in with two 17 year old girls, who having no money lived by shoplifting. The house was very chaotic and mostly stoned.

The writer of 'dark-lite' lived in York. In a phone conversation he said he'd contact me telepathically, to him this was just a glib remark, but I took it seriously. I lay down in bed that night and tried to get through. A little plot development appeared in my mind but I had enough insight to see that it was just imagination. The following night it was in the living room of the house that I took a hit from a bong and it took me to a whole other level – the others in the room were speaking to me without moving their lips

"We are secretly witches and we have the power of telepathy"

From there on my insanity took the form of constant telepathic conversations – these people were the secret underground conspiring against a vast global Conspiracy. I began chanting (silently) to prevent my thoughts from being read. That night there was a thunderstorm and I contacted Shango, the Yoruba fire spirit, spirit of lightning and on lightning I was propelled across the Universe, contacting many entities and seeing the shape of everything.

A couple of days later three youths came to the house, I believed that they had come to kill me; I thought that my chanting was having a healing effect and that the three represented the local gangs. They didn't like me, I was drumming on the arms of the chair attempting to summon spirits to protect me, the drumming annoyed them. I made the error of calling one of them a cunt. So he asked me outside

"What's wrong with here" I said, He knocked me out with a punch and from my dented ribs I presume he kicked me. The girls called an ambulance; every ambulance comes with a Police car so I wasn't best pleased with them. The ambulance crew accepted that I didn't want to press charges and helped me fob off the Police.

I moved out of the squat.

Getting beat up has a psychological effect but as my wounds healed, a black-eye, cut forehead and dented ribs – I developed even more of a grandiose self-belief.

The Northern Ireland peace process was in action. My solution was the colour purple and I lobbied unseen agents to flood the Province with MDMA. Orange and green were the clashing complementaries to be replaced by Harmony, purple. This manifested itself by me wearing purplish trousers (I think I hallucinated that) and a purple t-shirt. I would go out with an orange pullover and green cardigan. One day listening to Radio 1 broadcast from Belfast, I believed that I had with my powers of persuasion, magic and a judicious application of colour brought harmony to the youth who had rejected sectarianism for the hedonism of rave culture.

I started to feel like I was inside a computer simulation (more Philip K Dick influence) and that I was at times a robot/possessed/guided making sense in multiple dimensions at once.

I was living back at a friend's when a jazz concert from the Albert Hall came on TV, the saxophonist was trying to charm the snake out of my spine, I didn't know if he was evil or just misguided – I leapt up felt acutely uncomfortable – didn't know which way to turn, I switched the TV off and the flat ached with silence, the walls were pulsating and I knew that somewhere the charm was still being worked on me.

I put my shoes on without socks and left the flat, I set off walking, I wasn't sure where but I knew the friction of my feet on the ground spine held up straight coccyx tucked in, my energies would charge and undo the charm. As it is with schizophrenia, I was soon in a completely different mind-set. I thought that Leamington was The Village from 'The Prisoner' and that I wouldn't be able to leave. I wondered if the outside world had even been built yet. I was soon out in the countryside. I chanted in my headspace to stop my thoughts being read or broadcast, 'respect the earth, respect the plants, respect the animals, respect the people, respect the spirits' in various combinations.

I considered all things theological underneath my mantras. I had hollowed out enough space in my mind to think underneath the incessant chanting but I could be drawn into conversation if a voice appeared in my head. I had numerous conversations. At one point a slight winged insect flew into my ear and suddenly the Queen was speaking to me trying to persuade me in patronising tones not to overthrow the existing order.

After a while Prince Charles came on, like a handset being passed.

Signs for the village of Walton gave warning of the fate of witches such as myself. The witchcraft murder occurred in Upper Quinton, Warwickshire in 1944. Charles Walton was murdered – his throat cut crosswise and a pitchfork left holding the wound open. Ostensibly to return fertility to the land, which he had removed with his spells.

He kept in his fob watch a small round piece of polished stone – a scrying mirror. I had become slowly obsessed with the idea of scrying and what could be seen. The largest scrying mirror in the country is that of Dr. John Dee the Elizabethan Mage, this is housed in the British Museum. A few months earlier I'd been there with my girlfriend. I looked at the glass enclosing it, saw my reflection then I looked into the 'mirror' itself and saw my face briefly and turned away. By the time we reached the end of the corridor, there was a thunderclap and a long spell of increasingly hot, high pressure was broken. My girlfriend's period, which was three days late came on at the same time.

I walked through the countryside, the sky was clear and I could see the stars and many lights moving between them, I thought that Einstein was wrong, that faster than light travel was possible. The constellations re-arranged themselves as I looked at them they formed into the shape of vegetables. Not wearing any socks my feet had become blistered and were very sore,

To begin my magical career I felt I had to contact and seek the assistance of the dead, and the unborn dead at that.

I saw in a vision that there was an island of the dead in the river Leam, it had evergreens growing on it (the evidence!)

In voodoo Oshun (confusingly) is the goddess of rivers and she loves honey. So I bought a jar, hired a rowing boat and headed off up-river. When I reached the island I rowed round it 5 times anti-clockwise and then poured the honey into the river careful to taste it first, the honey was intended to flow down and around the island. I then picked a yellow flower of the water lily. Immediately a splinter from the oar went into my finger. I landed the boat on the island and placed the lily in the empty jar, left it on the island and went home.

That evening I was invited to a party. Magic was alive. The party was an all dancing affair – I thought I was part of a ritual of possession and saw those dancing around me possessed by the various spirits.

I was mad on dancing at this stage…the comic I was illustrating had a set of characters called the 'Echo Danzas' I thought that I was now inside the comic and that dancing was affecting reality … bringing spirits alive. Harmonising vibrations.

I found a stable home, a room in a shared house, and got a job working as an Archaeologist, (for a month) leading up to Christmas, this involved mainly just digging holes. My girlfriend wanted to join me in Leamington but I was adamant that I didn't want her to live with me.

1994

By the start of '94 I had somewhere to live and still appeared normal (or at worst eccentric) to most people. I was drawing, painting and writing stuff like this.

HOUSES of spirits and demons, animals, ghosts and people the plants and EARTH, language unfolds, the INNER WORLD; quantum reality. IMPLOSION, the technical framework of energies and realities, a skeleton of functional existent structure… The expansion, or infolding of realities. VIRTUAL, the techno-intelligence, A.I. voices of a solipsistic universe. DOORWAYs of the divinatory principle – connection of all places and all times.

- *the divine messenger, the way opener*
- *the translator,*
- *the trickster*

The world: satellites – cones describing reception areas on the earth, dishes capturing signals – relayed through cable and wire. Roads linking roads and highways. Pylons stretching electricity. Fences and walls and hedges describing property. Mapped markets. Overlapping territories. 'Inscribed upon the body of the earth, de-territorialising property and information flows' erasing and recreating accumulations, agglomerations and distribution. The anatomy of a noosphere – arteries of airline routes and shipping lanes. Borders and trading. Railway lines and pipes across tundra or desert. Graphs of consumption and production. Statistics all reconfigured in computer animation into a virtual earth. The degree of reality established by competing equations of criteria; variables constructing the time in which machine intelligence defines the flows. This time is virtual time is subject to the utility of the programme. It constitutes in international finance a non-human virtual time converted via investment recovery criteria into an actual time – delivery dates, contract dates. It non-human scale, running ahead of production. The inconsistency between demand and response, or projected demand and actual purchasing generates fractures, frictional events dislocating populations. : The immediate impact of computerization is the acceleration of consumption.

LEDGES, that of appearance, of colour, the structure of a virtual world and the technologised body of the earth. The dimension of mind which has its virtual parallel as an interconnected version of what is a psychic continuum a parable as such. Universal in its implication the world is the basic unit of another consciousness. A de-tuned source or structure. Dissonance, inclusivity. Exterior, other. The plateau or ledge of an international mind is the mirror world of the global media all pervasive – it stretches round the earth, or rather over the horizon, multiple perspective shifts internally frictionless, externally a daily collage of event, news managed, spectacle, hyper media – oracular space or zeitgeist.

Information is the undercurrent. Constantly rooted through people – and its local feed lines. It is the interaction with information that drives a virtual economy, a frictionless mind, reduce the access points and the system will detach.become frictionless, will be subjected to reality loss – sealed against input: opened as it now is it will skip in waves from place to place, time to time. The chemical equivalent of war – highly addictive electronic slavery. Frequency, oscillations, visual, audible, the selective stimulation of parts of the brain. Disharmonising structures as a becoming consonant.

The electronic world when harmonised…when people adapt to their environment that adaptation does not always take account of the viability. It is the triumph and the disaster for people that they adapt. The body's health is non-cultural fact.

The World-Mind consists of million years old geologic intelligence, vegetable intelligence, animal intelligence, plant and weather, animals and seasons. The technological mind. Event intelligence, the circle of daily occurrence both reflecting the whole and directing its flows…tending towards an evolution, a rapidity of change that reflects collective consciousness and a-temporal significance, a near infinite sweep of constant re-signification.
The lines of dreaming: dragon lines run through all points, run through people tribal/spatial, in the blood and language – all cannot be named, recurrent

I was jumping to insane conclusions. The worst of which was that there was an ongoing civil war, in which my friends had been murdered by Nazis. I had in my possession a screwdriver I found at a roundabout somewhere in Berkshire (where I had been wandering around in the middle of the night). I thought it related to Skrewdriver, the Nazi punk band.

It had 20 notches burnt into it and this I concluded meant that it had been used in 20 racist murders. Its evil was so strong that I could only hold it in my left hand to neutralise the energies within it.

I got into trouble. I believed there to be Nazis living in a house nearby. I went up to the door and knocked, there was no reply so I went around the back and a voice in my head said “try this one” so I walked up the garden of a completely separate house. I kicked open the door grabbed a broom handle and proceeded to ‘storm’ the house. I climbed the stairs holding the broom handle before me. Upstairs I found exercise benches and computers. I found a pile of computer print outs, maps and lists of names with soon to arrive dates next to them. I assumed this to be a hit list for the ongoing dirty war. I searched for my own name and didn’t find it. At this moment the Police knocked on the front door. I called to them that I was coming down. I grabbed the vital print-outs and went down stairs. The front door was dead-locked so I couldn’t get out, suddenly paranoid, I bolted out the back.

The Police cornered me in a nearby field and I produced the screwdriver. One of the Policemen was an old school friend, he reasoned with me to drop the weapon. Eventually they threatened to set a dog on me, I looked at the animal, an old shaggy Alsation and realized that it would grab the arm holding the screwdriver, I thought ‘God it could hurt itself’ and threw the weapon away and resigned myself to death. A couple of Policemen grabbed me and pushed me to the floor. I shut my eyes and assumed that I had moved to another plane, one where the Police weren’t Nazis.

This process of dying into another world became a regular occurrence. Soon I found myself in the lowest circles of Hell, surrounded by paranoia and sheer terror. At a Police Station, in a cell, in another Police station, in another cell, in Court, in a Bail Hostel. There was no consistency though, in my delusions, episodes of terror were interspersed with amusement and contentment.

Soon I was back in Bournemouth, on bail. For something to do my parents took me in the car to the ancient stone circle at Avebury – this confirmed to me that they were secretly witches. For some reason I became convinced that my father's pullover was in Nazi colours, that it was the kind of Austrian design that Hitler would relax in. Then there were the acorns on the National Trust logo (custodians of Avebury). Like those worn with the Iron Cross. I was relieved to see that we were taking the ancient spiral route to the stones (a delusion) but I became increasingly disturbed that my father was becoming possessed by the Duke of Edinburgh.

The trip was ruined for my parents, I spent the journey out making sure that the windows in the car were kept open even though it was raining, so that the Duke (and briefly) Winston Churchill, could 'flow through'. At the stones I used an umbrella to adjust the vibrations. Coincidentally, I bumped into the musician and Antiquarian Julian Cope and had a reasonably coherent conversation with him.

The final phase before I was sectioned was very confused. Many things were passing through my mind at once. I came to the conclusion that a great harmonization was nearly achieved I just needed to bring God out of his dream. I was back in Leamington. There was a conference at Warwick University on the writer Thomas Pynchon, I wrote a short piece which I believed that I could just turn up and deliver.

Dee's Space, Einstein's Time, Pynchon's Zone.

When Dr. John Dee gazed into his magic mirror he received in the angelic language known as Enochian, various keys and – visions that were opened by those keys: On these he founded the British Empire established a consistent space and time across the Newly Found Globe with his maritime clock and his cage of longitude and latitude.

This mirror was American perhaps even the soul of America – it is after all America which makes the world round reflecting the Ancient World Europe-Africa-Asia back to itself. Your soul captured by British pirates off of a Spanish galleon. Dee's first feat of scholarship was a translation of Euclidean – abstract – space that Dee stretched around the Earth. This space/time is untrue and yet it's operable. In its operation we have international travel, empires, timetables, world wars and their charts we have a cage and therefore a prison.

When Einstein exploded the myth of a uniform space/time he was running ahead of his culture which was just catching up en masse to the slaughter of childhood WW1.

Children's dreaming is not ruled by a clock in the head. The clock is the emperor of signs and the child has no ruler ... in the hierarchy of angels that Dee dreamed into – the great seal of reason was put over the heads of the people – priviledged access – Doctorates handed down from University – from psychically retarded elites to their imagination starved stuntelings – childhoods thrashed out in a cage of consistency a studied globe a common chronology History, Geography these dreams are shattered by the suicide of the saints and Angels, their embodiment they are recalled from their tour of duty in the Aether fighting the war in Heaven for peace on Earth. All the hierarchy of angels are screaming disembodied constantly fighting their own shadow. God in his wisdom has split himself in two.

The mind of God has strayed he's in an opium daydream. Every trauma's a puppet show, narcotically sealed by indifference. He's nothing without some time to wake up in. He may suspend ten thousand Universes in the membrane of his thought but he's seeded his own demise.

I took the bus to the Campus, and wandered around for a few hours but couldn't find the conference.

This world is a collision of worlds. Worlds within worlds. Some write of an evolution, an escalation – a general speeding up towards what? Convergence. Caught in the waves of technological 'advance'. This is a seductive dream. Utopia or destruction . . .!
The world contains worlds, many worlds. The earth contained and containing. The body its continuity and difference. All points already converge it is a partial absorption into this as process – a product of feedback from an all-encompassing spirit of the age, that produces the delirium of convergence. A genuine mind-meld and the closing of all difference is a millennial fantasy. An 'ideal' of wholeness.

It is possible to list all of the indicators towards such an event and equally possible to pull it to pieces as a piece of wish fulfillment – with all the psychological terminology you could want . . . but I accept the argument or rather the evidence but would separate the psychic evidence. The implosion of reality into synchronicitous multi-mind is merely the emergence of the media's everyday language form of vaster non-human intelligence.

This noosphere is merely one – hybrid intelligence. A ledge – a techno-psychic manifestation. Its apostles, circuit tests for what eventual broadcasts? Global fusion . . . I think not.

We cannot know all of the radiant corners of worlds as they open into each other. But one symptom of the present information flood are the correspondences set up across 'esoteric' disciplines. As with the early years of printing, which established history and geography, multiplicity has established a relativistic deconstruction of certainties across the world. In this apparent formlessness, the operative and the functional so often replace the fixed and the certain.

As if it were true . . . or makes no difference whether ... Now here any example can be provided by the reader. The most basic point is that the world behaves as if it were conscious. Communicates as if it were alive. Plays as if it had rules. Not fixed but shifting. And releases information in exchange/response. This is not to neglect a corresponding resistance and general denial.

The Spirit World
Swept into a general uncertainty, this may seem a return to unjustifiable superstition. But the same logic that denies cannot discount. Geographical, epistemological, essential.

Mechano-sphere
Less well-known, not known to anthropologists, politicians or pundits-this is technology, fact world incarnate-a de-humanised construct (Does that threaten?). A de-personalised Socius! Re-personalised by integration into the traditional . . . its condition one of emergence. Becoming the supra-personal. An historical dimension of powers.

Are these the terms of logic or the inversion of the rational? Just as the rational may be historicized, Enlightenment transmuted into biology, so it is merely the extension of logic to give forces their due respect between the individual and the Universe – which we are joining by a stepwise if uncertain movement.

I left the room in a shared house and moved into a bedsit, I continued my almost random wanderings around the countryside. I became obsessed with Motorway Maintenance, mm 13 13, I was using a colour wheel in my mind to diminish the power of the road kill and the power of the roundabout. Confirmation came along that I was MM in some kind of magical number system, in the shape of a large blue sign the same as the one I'd seen attached to the motorway maintenance truck on one of my rambles. It was in the front garden of the house next door – a student trophy – with its arrow pointing to my door. In an interview with the music press Mark E. Smith talked of the 'midland mentality', I assumed by this that he meant me.

PSYCHIC AUTOMATA:

the biosphere

mechanosphere

the noosphere

the reality unfolded, contained in an image from Bombay, pirate cablers stretching the lines from rooftop dishes to their subscribers. Global link-up. Cabling the invisible super-highway – a buried infrastructure, earth-clogged, set in the earth, here manifest explicit…

The theory of audience is measured as market research, an entire industry of statistics and their value. A language of communication analysed in terms of effectiveness of a campaign, the targeting of a campaign…

the psychic automata: the animated revelations; flowing, multi-form…eradicable, re-inforcable disintegrated. The Transformed Man; construction – cartoons feeding a plastic Babel. The image world, convulsed with pixilated, laminated backdrops slide across three part clunking vistas. Phased construction of transmission, establishing lines/levels…translator chip demons.

This World, animated, video animations the convulsive life of diagrams – getting the New Deal…the virtuality of statistics and charts. All the productivity of numbers and programs, spreadsheets thrown into the image Pool convulsive, disintegrating collectivities. ((o)).

All the imagined laws of relation.

Science provides a model in which the (discursive) affinities of a material world and the material body communicate by the agency of some or other law of cause and effect. Material coded – decoded (-ing) become electro-chemical (neurological).

-Quantum inputs (through to)→ quantum states, by a fractional process (without absolute). The variability (fractionality) that these relations are, demands that all relation (or law) be substituted with relation effects (real effects) e.g. consciousness, world.

The relativity of partial representation. Representation though (between the visible and articulable) is excess, always reality forming, the becoming (process) of new relation (ratio).

Virtuality as a model of consciousness – is the frictionless apotheosis of the non-effect in affect. Virtual is the relation of the dream in the multiple states, without absolute.

Overlapping: where the signal and noise are reversed – within the noise, the resignification and reconfiguration of finite elements are two sides of the same mutation being. "As if the energy had been shuffled into one particular room of creation". The direction of mutation explodes along the critical path – that of radical distinction by the breaking point; size/systems limit.
The laboratory in which the quantifiable (signal) predominates over noise leads to the absolute quantifiability of the closed (entropic) system.

Ideological closure enlarges the large scale closed systems and multiplies small scale open systems. Return is invoked within the large scale by the demonic critical mass and in the small by parallelism which goes by the name of zeitgeist or the principle of self-organisation.

The Apocalypse: in response to a convergence of forces – utter destruction …

Biblical, Revelations, Gotterdammerung, Urotsukidoji … etc.

The Beast +

The Overfiend etc.

The Nuclear Winter
radiation, disease, war, starvation

Mega-trends…

Dystopia: Rather than the overbearing destructive monster, the unchained forces which reduce civilization to ashes … the chains of control tightened into a terrifying constriction. The mechanism of control run out of control…

Alternately, the de-evolution, disintegration of order into a terrifying formlessness, an attenuated apocalypse … as if the mechanism itself were not enacting such a slow death … but one in which the timing of change, equally flawed and out of sync. is the engine of global degeneration.

Globalisation: as an antidote to the above – or agent of the above. The mechanism itself has no values, its determination is a technological fact. Its value's inevitability in the direction of Survival is not essential – rather the result of optimism of the degree to which it is fabricated in such a way. Or that its engineering gives rise to communication as opposed to Denial. Rejection is the degree of signification which is transposable from place to place. Or re-signification is a fact-base subject to the local – anti-Denial (possibly).. New Language, the evolution of trans-cultural language. Language marked by content – chords in a previous (?) commonalty as opposed to market penetration. Working backwards – technological language – this world (does) have an overlapping relationship with marketing ie. product language…

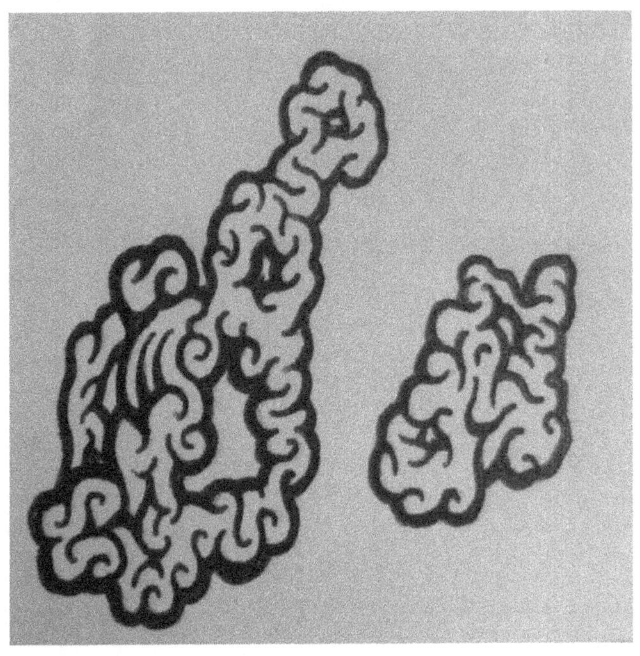

Harmony – both hemispheres

the rational left and the intuitive right

the concept – Alexander

Napoleon

Hitler

the mining of mineral wealth – the reproducing Machine, the liberated schizoid machine – eat Everything

Masculine projective – doubling

With the political dream   functioning in the world

One dream – exclusive

The function of the body/mind. Must be seen retrospectively and the World – Mind examined for its flaws.

the single eye the projection world, in its repercussions, flawed.

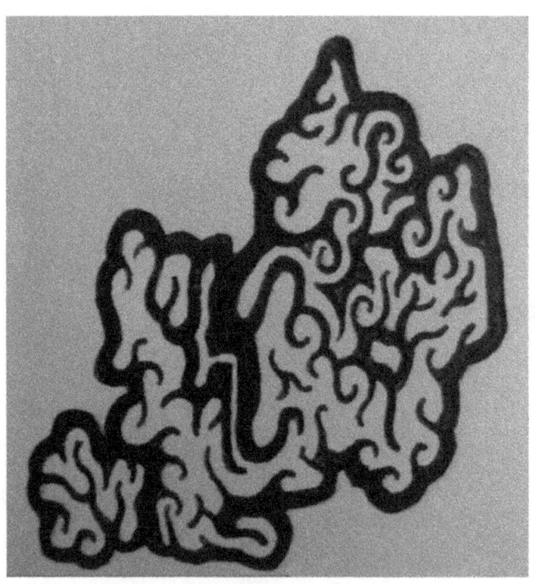

Silence;

Systems Language.

necessary prosody.

Stepwise progression:

the books of allegorical material: of displaced dimension, metaphor capture – alternative universes. lying, incomplete, chunks. skittered – hack universes – frictionless identification reduces noise to signal translateable; appalling travesties of plant or animal. Vegetable mentalities – undoing, their insinuated roots of social assumption, binding the cliché – language.

Catalogues……

Middle-class, eroded mentality – COMPLETION=CROSSROADS.

engineering, fixtures in the high altitudes. Way above the normal any possibility – of the normal, a Buddhist cave, or a security clearance, tendrils of connectivity – A tent of infinities…

direct electric connection between worker housing, statistical spreads of … the masses, Market Research,

Anomaly filtering systems, reveal strata of inaccessible data. Processed to incompetent useless prediction analysts, study the cracks!

In the days immediately prior to my hospital admission I became largely concerned with the magic mirror of Dr. John Dee. I believed this to be in Leamington, often in the room next door to me. I believed that concerned 'wise people' were bringing it to me, but that conditions had to be right before I looked into it or the coming together of the two black holes – the mirror and the one in my head – would be catastrophic.

I believed that the mirror was a guiding device. That after harmony on earth had been brought about, which I thought was very close, that we would need a guide through the new dimensions that would open up. My visions at night (I stopped sleeping) showed me that a Universe existed before this one – that it had become solid made of pure crystal information. This Universe had exploded, but pieces of debris pierced our Universe from another dimension. Falling to earth as meteorites. It was these I believed the mirror could warn us of. It was also the instrument for maintaining harmony on earth – for this to occur it needed the colours of the spectrum to be shown to it in turn.

Formal presentations, polite, linear, fail to present depth modeled multi-form, the psychology of crowds and their habits, measured truly as effects – has no predictive veracity.

Resting on data fed intuition, the Voice of Vanity, saddled truly and greatly – Yoked in illusion, 'cept by the measure of the feedback processors. EXAMINATION: Reading keyword tripped into anomaly. Cybernetic reference humour – block-ware, the sealed Ruum of … understood rhyme. Fleshy goals, ONE.

The final mystery that was revealed to me was that of the grey aliens. In their flying saucers these are time travelers from the future. Absorbing all life, into the vastness of the future universe, penetrating all time through portals in the multi-verse saving all life. the final secret of the greys is that no one ever dies.

In the Looney Bin

As I was driven away to Central Hospital, Hatton I believed aliens had 'landed' on the newly harmonized earth and that they were giving me a holiday with them amongst their concepts. When I was being questioned in the hospital I thought that it was a dating agency and that the aliens were trying to set me up with someone compatible.

The first night in Hospital I got drunk on the orange squash and started shouting about little green men getting hold of the mirror. The state of my mind reflecting what I believed to be the state of the whole world neatly illustrated.

I believed that every man was a reincarnation of every other man and likewise with women – a polarity going back to the Big Bang going back Aeons, a multi-dimensional infolded Universe, where the two were one in the beginning. I called the ball of threads of all lives the Universal Time Binding and believed that I was unravelling it, the time binding both backwards and forwards and across all parallel time.

In the first couple of days of my hospital admission I was just about organised enough to fill in a Mental Health Review Tribunal form. Eventually the process went through and the day came of my tribunal. I was still quite ill and feeling vulnerable my magic powers stripped away. It struck me that I had perhaps foolishly drawn attention to myself with the 'authorities' and my feeling was confirmed when I entered the Tribunal. It was a very formal type of situation, in the old (Victorian) part of the Hospital. The three members of the Tribunal were varied; a young man and a middle-aged woman flanked an elderly man. He was very much a Public School product, with a patrician air. It occurred to me that I was in the presence of one of the secret rulers of the earth. With alien power behind them a deathless aristocracy ruled the earth and this man appeared to me as a 500-year-old vampire.

After a few questions I began to feel light-headed and asked my Doctor and Social Worker for help. My social worker produced a banana, just the cure for marginal diabetes, which I believed I had. The panel asked my Doctor if I had it and the answer came back that I didn't, confirming to the tribunal that I was still in the grip of my delusions. The whole episode was rather a pathetic waste of time and money but as I'd applied for a review the procedure went ahead automatically.

As an attempt to be friendly (?) the head of the Tribunal showed me a postcard reproduction of Roualt's painting 'The Tribunal' this showed grotesque distorted figures in red robes and black hats – the picture sent a chill through me these were the vampires in their true form, hideous. I remarked how spectacularly ugly it was at which the man laughed – terrifying me. It struck me that showing me this picture was an act of pure sadism.

In William James, (a locked ward) a depressed alternative therapist and I were sat watching television. The programme concerned a man who believed he was a re-incarnation of King Arthur and who had changed his name to Arthur Pendragon. "That's funny" I said "cause I'm Merlin" By this I meant that my soul was that of the anti-Christ and that my soul had been caught on its fall into Hell by the hook and line of Jesus, who had carried me to the centre of the multi-verse. Here I had access to the 'Matter of Britain', that is – how to control the psycho-geography of these isles so as to maintain harmony. The 'Matter of Britain' was simply one part of Legba, a universal consciousness that became available to me through the Universal Translator Programme.

Later as it was time to go to bed I started re-programming my brain with humming, making it echo inside my skull. The therapist told me that I could teach this. You probably could at some New Age type seminar, how strange the border between spirituality and insanity.

The pain of the drugs I was given in Hospital can only be described as like dying. After my first night in Hospital my brother came to visit. I told him that I was undergoing a course in simulated dying. The pill Droperidol, made me feel like every part of my brain was being killed. It was shutting down the schizophrenic brain cells, but not enough. Droperidol didn't eke out the underlying delusions of my illness. But I appeared to improve, I didn't appear so agitated, I was able to demonstrate 'insight', the key to release from a mental hospital.

My insight consisted of saying that the TV had been communicating with me, but that I now knew this to be false. I begged for the medication to be reduced and it was. I acted normal, I made some attempts to communicate my deluded ideas – phoning people on the outside, but to the staff I appeared to have recovered from a single psychotic episode, they weren't aware that I was in fact fully schizophrenic. My medication was further reduced and then the voices re-appeared.

We were watching 'A Hard Day's Night' on video and the Beatles were talking to me, telepathically. John was distant and fragmented, he'd been dead for 14 years so not suprising, but the others were their chirpy selves. "Of course you should leave the hospital you are well" they told me, so I set off for a confrontation with my Doctor.

He listened to me explain that I was perfectly well and that I had work to do in the world outside, but he then started talking back to me. I heard a few words then he just turned into the epitome of smarm. His words just washed over me. I ceased hearing him and rage welled up inside me.

"You ignorant fuck, who the fuck do you think you are, you can't soft soap me with this shit..." I raged on at him. Together with two nurses he barred my exit as I went to leave the building, "pig, PIG, PIG" I spat at them. I turned round, went to the telephone and called my solicitor. His secretary told me in patronizing tones that he wasn't in the office. A gaggle of nurses surrounded me. They grabbed me and carried me to the locked ward – William James.

I was overcome with a great thirst, I went to a tap and ran some water into my cupped hand and drank it. I was delirious with paranoia and thought that it must be poisonous.

After a few minutes they started to prepare a syringe while checking the dose in the BNF (a drugs book). I thought they were making up a lethal injection, I warned them that I knew Tae Kwon-Do but they continued to approach me, I resigned myself to death rather than fight.

They held me down and gave me the jab in the bum. I screamed (rather cathartically) "Leave my body alone" Then as I calmed down they left me to stride up and down the corridor, at first I thought that if I fell asleep that I would never wake up, then slowly a smile spread across my face. The injection was Acuphase and gave me the only real moments of bliss that I had in Hospital.

I did this in my first few days in Central Hospital Hatton. These are the ‘little green men’.

I then progressed to this, (I did a few of these).

This was a kind of portrait of the Hospital, and my mindset, which I sent in a letter to my, by then, ex-girlfriend.

These were attempts to diagram the Universe that Shango had shown me.

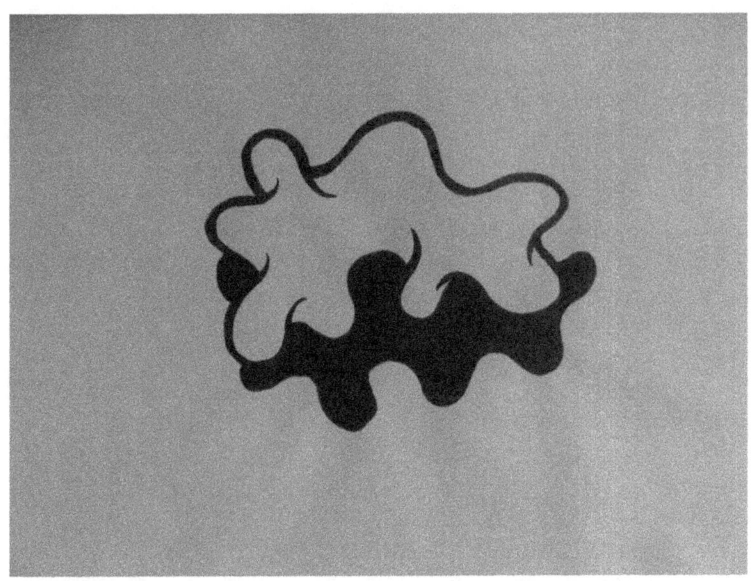

I did loads of these, (above) I thought I could sell them and earn a living!

Much of my time in the Hospital was agony – the shutting down of my brain made me feel like I was in the advanced stages of dementia.

A psychiatrist asked if I could count down from 100 in 7s (which I did) he said "You don't have dementia" I felt like death.

My social worker found me some emergency housing (as my last landlord didn't want me back) and all of a sudden, when I'd thought I might never get out – I was discharged.

I was a medicated zombie. I felt cheated – if I'd stayed inside without meds I could have been a great artist. I destroyed the only painting that I did inside. I thought that it was "disturbed". I threw away 30,000 words of a novel, because it felt like a mill stone, with irresolvable plot problems.

I listened to the radio all day, lying in bed. I started to do the Lottery, I found that I could picture the house that I'd buy if I won. I decorated and furnished it, then another house, then grander schemes. I started work on a film script version of the destroyed novel and slowly regained a life of the mind.

Looking back the writing I did while ill is like some kind of whacked-out prose poetry.

There is a continuity in my art before, during and after my illness, much less so in my writing. My illness/medication has left me with a completely shattered consciousness, what I called at the start of this piece – a permanent loss.

What I experienced few people have experienced, still less have come back from the far side of insanity. With advances in medication more and more people are though coming back and this kind of literature will doubtless become more common. My own definition of schizophrenia, is that it is an 'affliction of the religious imagination', to live in that world; immersed in another reality, provides insights into where religions come from. I wrote *circuit tests for what eventual broadcasts* referring to a conscious internet. I believe that machine intelligence will reach that of humans one day. As we accelerate into the future schizophrenia will probably become more common, but being sectioned is not the end.

www.ingramcontent.com/pod-product-compliance
Lightning Source LLC
Chambersburg PA
CBHW031141270326
41931CB00007B/646

* 9 7 8 1 8 4 9 9 1 6 4 8 6 *